THE
Old Photographs
SERIES

BATTERSEA AND CLAPHAM

St Mary's church, Clapham Park Road, c. 1905.

THE
Old Photographs
SERIES

BATTERSEA
AND CLAPHAM

Compiled by
Patrick Loobey

CHALFORD

BATH • AUGUSTA • RENNES

First published 1994
Copyright © Patrick Loobey, 1994

The Chalford Publishing Company Limited
St Mary's Mill, Chalford, Stroud
Gloucestershire GL6 8NX

ISBN 0 7524 0010 X

Typesetting and origination by
Alan Sutton Limited
Printed in Great Britain

Contents

Introduction   7

1.   Clapham High Street   9

2.   Clapham Old Town   15

3.   South Clapham Streets   19

4.   North Clapham Streets   29

5.   Clapham Buildings   41

6.   Clapham Common   53

7.   Battersea – Clapham Junction   61

8.   Battersea – Old Town   77

9.   Battersea – Buildings and People   87

10. Battersea Streets   103

11. Battersea Park   115

Clapham High Street, c. 1905.

Clapham Common, c. 1912.

Introduction

The story that unfolds through the medium of the photographs in this book is of the expansion of two small Surrey villages throughout the sixty-three-year reign of Queen Victoria and beyond into the twentieth century.

Clapham was home to wealthy city merchants during the eighteenth century, and the magnet for a group of Christian gentlemen, the Clapham Sect, who were less interested in their own position in life than in the freedom of slaves.

Battersea was a backwater until the arrival of the railways in 1838 and the attendant need for housing. Only 801 houses with 4,764 people were listed in 1837, but the opening of the misnamed "Clapham" Junction, having rail connections with the City and West End, was the greatest spur to development over the next thirty years.

Prior to the formation of local councils, the Parish Vestries oversaw the democratic repair of roads and the digging of drainage ditches, ensured the poor and infirm were looked after, and appointed constables to lock up miscreants (the last recorded use for the stocks by St Mary's church was in 1821).

Clapham was to change dramatically with the London County Council redeveloping much of the Wandsworth Road and Clapham Park districts. In addition Clapham and the Nine Elms area suffered badly during the second world war.

The author would be pleased to hear from any person with memories or comments they wish to share regarding the scenes within these pages.

P.J. Loobey
231 Mitcham Lane
Streatham
SW16 6PY

Clapham Junction, c.1908.

Born in 1947, Patrick Loobey has lived in Balham, Putney, Southfields and Streatham – all within the Borough of Wandsworth. He joined Wandsworth Historical Society (founded 1953) in 1969 and has served on its archaeological, publishing and management committees, being chairman of the society from 1991 to 1994. Having collected Edwardian postcards of Wandsworth Borough and the surrounding district for nineteen years, he has a wide-ranging collection, encompassing many local roads and subjects.

Patrick privately published a volume of postcard views of Putney and Roehampton in 1988 and another on Battersea in 1990. Forthcoming titles will include Streatham, Balham and Tooting, Wandsworth, Putney and several other areas.

Reproductions of all the views in this book are available from Patrick Loobey, 231 Mitcham Lane, Streatham, London, SW16 6PY (081 769 0072).

The captions to the photographs in this book are but a brief glimpse into the varied and complex history of the area. For those seeking further information the Wandsworth Historical Society covers the borough's boundaries, publishing a journal and various papers, the fruits of members' research. Monthly meetings are held on the last Friday of each month at 8p.m. at the Friends' Meeting House, Wandsworth High Street.

The author must thank and recommend the Local History Library at Lavender Hill, Battersea, where early newspapers, deeds, directories, maps and parish records are made available to those wishing to research names, dates and addresses of families or business concerns.

8

One
Clapham High Street

Clapham clock tower, c. 1910. Many of our local monuments were donated at the turn of this century by local worthies, and the clock tower was paid for by Alexander Glegg, Mayor of Wandsworth 1905-1906.

The clock tower was a major tram stop and interchange for bus routes at this junction where, in 1930, we can see a tram inspector and passengers waiting by the tram stop.

The unveiling ceremony of the clock, 19th July 1906, was undertaken by the Lord Mayor of London, Sir Walter Vaughan Morgan, a director of Morgan Crucibles large factory on Battersea's waterfront. Accompanied by the Sherrifs, he drove in state from the City to Clapham, where the Mayor of Wandsworth, councillors and invited guests attended.

Clapham High Street, c. 1912. The City and South London Railway was extended from Stockwell to Clapham on 3rd June 1900, and this station remained in use until 1926 when the Northern Line was extended to Balham. The booking hall was moved to its present position beside the clock tower. The original station was eventually demolished in March 1930.

Clapham High Street, c. 1930. A popular and busy shopping area that has not attracted any of the vast emporiums seen elsewhere; The Majestic cinema on the left beyond the bus is now a nightclub. The Wesleyan Methodist church on the right was destroyed during the second world war and the foundation stone of the new church was laid down on 8th October 1960.

Flags and bunting suspended across Clapham High Street from specially erected poles greet visitors in the weeks preceeding Christmas 1909.

The Two Brewers public house, Clapham High Street, c. 1912. Notice the massive gas lamps hanging from cast iron brackets which were removed from this and other pubs at the beginning of the last war. The building is now used as a nightclub.

J. W. Clark, Jeweller, 104 High Street, Clapham, about 1907, on the corner of Manor Street. A close look at the single storey shops on this side of the High Street will reveal they have been placed in front of eighteenth-century houses.

Clapham High Street, c. 1908. The shop blinds are out to protect the goods on display which would suffer discoloration from sunlight if not shielded. Ladies were not seen out of doors without a hat before the first world war

Clapham Road, c. 1912. To the right is the Bedford Arms public house, rebuilt during the 1930's and fully refurbished in 1994. The Clapham Auction Rooms and the small post office stand at the beginning of the High Street.

The Post and Telegraph office, 8 High Street, run by Mr Walker in 1910, also served up tea cakes and chocolate. The Royal Oak public house, rebuilt in the 1930's, now occupies 8 and 10 High Street. Mr Barker is seen in the doorway of his meat and provisions shop where sausage rolls were 1d and steak and kidney pies cost 2d each.

Two
Clapham Old Town

The Old Town in 1912 was overlooked by the spire of the Congregational church which was erected in 1851 but damaged by a flying bomb in 1944 and eventually demolished in 1954. The three storey building is the Sun public house. The longer row to the left, listed as newly built in 1707, probably contains some of the oldest surviving buildings in Clapham.

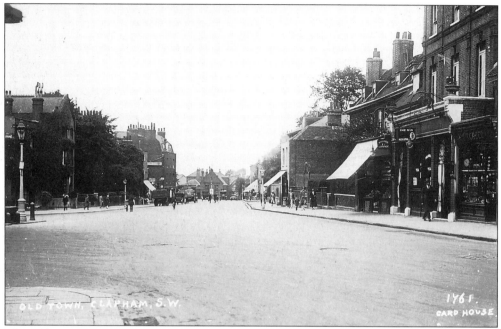

The Old Town in 1930, with the Sun public house on the right. In the far distance is the former parochial school, built on land granted by the Lord of the Manor, Richard Atkins, in 1648. The two properties in the centre of the lower photograph were demolished for the construction in 1939 of Maritime House, headquarters of the National Union of Seamen. The fire station of 1902 is on the left.

The Old Town in 1906 had barely changed in 200 years. The parochial school, on the left, was built in 1809 by public subscription and rebuilt in 1887. Lydon Road is just beyond the barbers shop on the right, which had an exceptionally large barbers pole overhanging the roadway by approximately 12 to 15 feet.

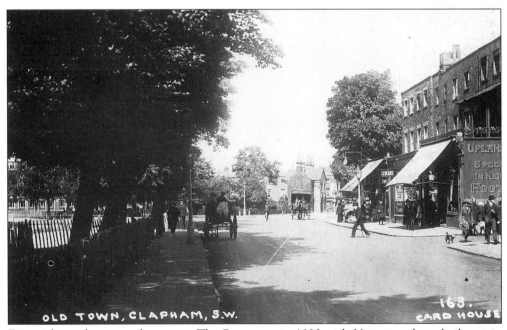

Fine eighteenth-century houses on The Pavement in 1930 with Victorian shops built out in front of the ground floor elevations. The old fire station of 1869, beyond the horse and cart, became disused when the L.C.C. built the new fire station in 1902 and is now a private residence.

Holy Trinity parish church (c. 1915) dates from 1774 when it replaced the twelfth-century parish church that stood in Rectory Grove. A large plaque on the south wall commemorates the abolition of slavery and those of the Clapham sect that brought it about, Thornton, Venn, Charles Grant, Macauley and Wilberforce. Large splinters to the plaque are due to wartime bombing. The stretch of water is the Cock pond, created when gravel was dug for use in construction of the church.

The Pavement in 1910 had a variety of tradesmen such as Hellis & Sons, photographers, Farnell, who practised in English and American dentistry, and Stringer & Bird, purveyors of fancy goods. Zachary Macauley and his famous son lived at No.5 and a plaque to their memory is fixed to the first floor frontage.

Three
South Clapham Streets

Crescent Grove, c. 1908. This group of buildings has housed several authors, amongst them Borden Maxwell, who wrote on various aspects of London's history, and also the art critic W.H.J. Weale.

SOUTH SIDE, CLAPHAM COMMON. S.W.
(c. 8.
CARD HC

Southside, 3rd March 1909. Local authorities used the unemployed to clear away snow and large banks of it were formed on the roadside. Gideon Mantell moved to Crescent Lodge, the left-most of the two large houses, in 1838. His interest in geology led him to collect a famous collection of fossils, many of which are now in the British Museum; he also formed the Clapham Atheneum, a scientific society.

Convent of Notre Dame, South Side, c. 1930. Originally the family home of John Thornton, who gathered together the Clapham sect at the end of the eighteenth century, the mansion was a convent school from 1851 to 1939. The 12½ acre estate was purchased by Wandsworth council in 1942, with the first part of the new housing estate opening on 30th July 1947. The run-down buildings were used for temporary shelter for the homeless in the immediate postwar period (the author and his parents were placed there in 1948). The convent and mansion were cleared away the same year and the Palladian orangery of 1793 is now the only surviving remnant of the Thornton home.

Deauville Road, c. 1910, renamed Elms Crescent by the L.C.C. Development commenced in 1892 (with the small houses adjoining Elms Road) and completed during the 1920's with the blocks of flats at the corner of Rodenhurst Road.

Narbonne Avenue, c. 1908, developed during the 1890's on the site of Eagle House, where Mr Edgar, of the Swan & Edgar department store, lived at the end of the nineteenth century. This was also the residence of Samuel Smith, great grandfather of Florence Nightingale.

Lynette Avenue, c. 1925. The road name was approved in 1885 and building started in 1886 with the construction of six villas on the south side of the road.

Junction of Southside and Cavendish Road in 1926, with a succession of L.C.C. trams en route to Tooting. Cavendish House, demolished in 1905, the home and laboratory of Henry Cavendish, the eminent chemist, stood on the corner of Dragmire Lane, which was later renamed Cavendish Road to commemorate the famous man who calculated the weight of the Earth. The milestone still points the way to London.

Abbeville Road in 1908 appears to be a safe playground for children. The pavement pump to the left was used for filling horse-drawn wagons employed by the local council to damp down the dust of the gravel road surfaces.

Abbeville Road, c. 1914. Mr Mountford ran the Post Office and stationery shop whose windows are covered in local postcard views that he published. Oil jars as seen above Odell & Co.'s hardware and oil shop are rare sites today, although seven survive above a corner shop in the Polygon, Old Town, Clapham.

Golding Brothers at 35 Abbeville Road in 1907 appear able to supply many services to local householders such as coal, flour, dog biscuits and house removals. Mr Golding, seen here, had sent his two sons on holiday to his sister's house in Exminster and was hoping they were not too much of a worry; he was getting on "A1".

No. 168 Clapham Park Road, c. 1910, the family home of Mr Robert Martin from the turn of the century to at least 1916. Few of these houses survived the wholesale demolition and local authority housing developments of the 1930's and 1940's.

Junction of Clarence Road and Poynders Road, 3rd March 1909. A recent snow blizzard has left the roads with a blanket of snow that horse-drawn traffic would not clear as quickly as motor transport can today. Admirable local authority initiative placed street names on the lamp posts. Mr George Balls, Veterinary Surgeon, lived at The Warren on this corner; other house names were The Heathers, St Tudno, Borrowdale and Kemsing.

King's Avenue, Clapham Park, c. 1912. Alexander Glegg, Mayor of Wandsworth 1905-1906, lived at Craig Owen, 89 King's Avenue. Before the 1965 reorganisation of local councils Clapham and Streatham were both administered by Wandsworth Borough Council.

Atkins Road, c. 1912. Henry Atkins, physician to James I, purchased the manor of Clapham in 1616 for £6,000 and the family retained it for the next two hundred years. The white marble monuments of the 1690's to Sir Richard Atkins and his family were rediscovered in 1885 and are now on view in St Paul's church. The music hall comedian Dan Leno lived at Springfield in Atkins Road.

Clapham Park Road at the junction with Park Hill in 1912. This old trackway between Clapham and Brixton retains the original Acre Lane name along the eastern portion of the road. It was renamed when Thomas Cubitt redeveloped the area. The shops were demolished for road widening during the 1960's.

Clapham Park Road, c. 1903. The King's Head public house with St Mary's church in the far distance. Earlier short-lived names for this short stretch of road were South Road and Loats Road, after Mr Loat, a builder from Balham Hill. The Clapham Park estate of 250 acres was developed from 1825 by Mr Thomas Cubitt. who no doubt expected a similar success to that of his project in Belgravia.

Clapham Park Road, c. 1910. The Catholic church of St Mary, built in 1851, looms above the mid-Victorian shops lining the street. The Gardener's Arms public house, on the right, a seventeenth-century building, has been demolished. Children's iron hoops are on display at The Bazaar on the corner of Carfax Square, where servants could register free for work in the larger houses nearby. The William Bonney housing estate now occupies the area up to The Auld Triangle public house on the right.

Four
North Clapham Streets

The Chase, c. 1912. In 1666 the Gaudon estate of 432 acres extended from Wandsworth Road up to the common where, in the area of Victoria Rise, the house in which (in 1703) Samuel Pepys died was built in 1663. The road was laid out in the 1880's and the name suggests the seventeenth-century hunting grounds of the old estate. The Coleman family, of mustard fame, lived at No. 32 and later in Crescent Grove.

The Cedars, North Side, Clapham Common, c. 1925. The Cedars, a country mansion erected in 1718 on part of the Gaudon estate, was demolished in 1864 to make way for Cedars Road and the erection of these two grand blocks designed by the architect J.T. Knowles. The Cedars, once used by Battersea Polytechnic as housing for female students, is now The Parkside Hotel.

Cedars Road looking north towards the Wandsworth Road in 1910. St Saviour's church, stands proudly amongst the houses erected in the 1860's and 1870's. In 1917 No. 19 was St Edward's Convent, and No 35 was St Faith's home for deaf and dumb girls. Archibald Dawney, mayor of Wandsworth from 1908 to 1918, lived at No 4 until his death in 1919. No 18 was the Helenen Heigm orphanage.

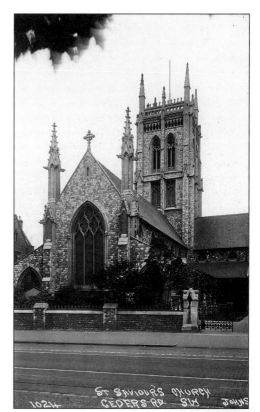

St Saviours' church, Cedar's Road, c. 1912. Built in 1864 at a cost of £4,000, styled in French Gothic from designs by J.T. Knowles, it was concecrated by Bishop Wilberforce, son of the emancipator. The church seated 700 and survived up to 1940, when bombed. J.T. Knowles, celebrated architect who designed many of the local churches, lived at The Hollies, 31 North Side.

Victoria Road, c. 1910, renamed Victoria Rise by the L.C.C. Where the road meets the common was the country villa, built in 1753, of Henry Hoare, member of the bank of that name. Adorned with "pleasure grounds and gardens laid with great taste and judgement" and painted internal features, the house was demolished in 1851 and the land laid out for development for these large terraces. Mrs Gorringe of the West End store lived at No. 7.

Bromfelde Road, c. 1912. The celebrated illustrator of medical books M.H. Lapidge moved from No. 43 Old Town to No. 69 Bromfelde Road in 1903, but moved from the district six years later. Miss E. Wood ran a private nursing home at Nos 90 and 92 in 1916.

Edgeley Road, c. 1908. Samuel Edgeley was vicar of Wandsworth parish church; he died on 21st March 1732 aged 73 and is buried in a vault at Clapham parish church. He is described as "vicar of Wandsworth parish for 44 years, an excellent preacher, an honest worthy clergyman, sociable, generous and charitable". The small building on the right was the L.C.C. (Clapham) school of art; the principal was Leonard Charles Nightingale. It was renamed the Hugh Walker Centre for "community education" on 30th October 1987 after the chairman of the governors from 1978 to 1985. The school bell still hangs in the entrance.

Orlando Road, c. 1912. In 1840 Orlando Jones invented a process by which starch could be made from rice. In 1848 Orlando Jones & Co. built a factory in York Road, Battersea with a frontage to the river. Messrs Coleman, mustard manufacturers, bought out the firm in 1901 and transferred the works to Norwich.

Turret Grove, c. 1910. Little has changed in this scene today. The Elizabethan manor house that stood in Rectory Grove until 1837 had at one end a five storey turret with cupola that gives the road.

Manor Street, c. 1912. The Bowyers Arms public house at No. 68, at the far end of this view, was built in 1846 by Thomas Cubbitt. William Henry Cory, whose family lived at No. 10, was one of the 600 that rode in the ill-fated Charge of the Light Brigade at Balaclava in October 1854 during the Crimean War. The Clapham Baths in Manor Street was opened on 7th July 1932 by Prince George, later Duke of Kent, and the Mayor of Wandsworth, Councillor Lieutenant-Colonel A. Bellamy.

Larkhall Rise, c. 1912. Edgeley Road is on the immediate left and Manor Street just beyond the horse and cart. Cardinal Bourne, Arhbishop of Westminster, was born at No. 5 Larkhall Rise on 23rd March 1861, and died on 1st January 1935. His rise in the church was most extraordinary: ordained at St Mary's, Clapham Park Road, bishop at 35, archbishop at 42 and cardinal by 50. His mother moved to 20 Grafton Square, Clapham and her son would often come to see her in Clapham.

Larkhall Rise, c. 1912. Albion Road is to the left, with three policemen posing for the cameraman, Mr R.J. Johns of Longley Road, Tooting, before moving off on their separate beats. Houses on the left were demolished by the L.C.C. during the 1930's and replaced by the Springfield housing estate which opened shortly before the second world war.

The Duke of York public house, Larkhall Lane, a small Victorian hostelry, was demolished, rebuilt and reopened in 1940. Best's brewery, on the right, was taken over by Frost's factory producing sausages and pies. The Gunter Arms public house, further along, and the other buildings all made way in the 1930's for large-scale housing development by the L.C.C. that reaches to the Wandsworth Road.

Larkhall Lane, c. 1912. Jeffrey's Road is to the right. The building on the left is The Larkhall Tavern, which now stands amidst council flats and the Allen Edwards primary school erected since the war. The Larkhall Tea Gardens are noted on Wyld's map of 1844. A small watercourse ran from Elwell Street between Nos 106-108 Larkhall Lane and onwards to the Wandsworth Road.

Lillieshall Road, c. 1912, late eighteenth-century dwelling houses for artisans that still survive in little altered condition. The public house on the corner of North Street, originally registered as a beer house and run by James Funnel in 1901 and Mrs Mary Hislop in 1916, was given the name "Tim Bobbin", possibly after the Lancashire painter and poet of that name.

Braybourne Avenue, c. 1912. We have an extraordinary coincidence of surnames listed as residents in 1902 for the following are given: Mr Edwin Pentecost lived at No. 15, Mr Lewis Bottle at No. 17, John Henry Perfect at No. 19, Edward Idle at No. 23, Thomas Wright at No. 10, Mrs Trail at No. 42, Edward Rivers at No. 48, William Payne at No. 54, and a Mr Potter at No. 60.

Wandsworth Road Station, c. 1912. The road was lowered under the bridge in 1909 to accommodate the introduction of the electric trams. The Lord Raglan public house, renamed The Horseshoe, stands on the corner of Pensbury Place, then named Thurlow Road. Mr Atkins' shoe repairers, on the corner of Pensbury Street to the right, resoled gents' shoes for 2s 6d and ladies' shoes for 1s 6d.

Wandsworth Road Station, c. 1912. The station, built for the London Chatham and Dover Railway Co., was opened in March 1863. The London Brighton and South Coast Railway Co. used the two platforms to the left and electrified their suburban services in 1908, while the L.C.D.R. closed their half in 1916.

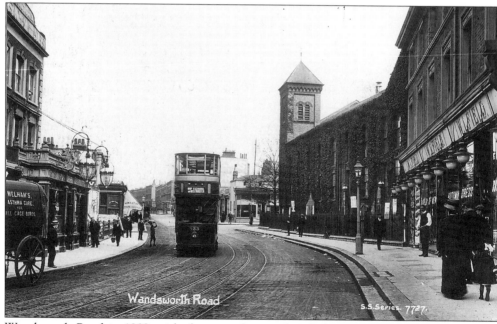

Wandsworth Road in 1909, with the recently introduced electric trams, the service having started in September 1909. The Victoria Tavern of the 1870's still serves beer and traditional cheer, while the Victoria chapel, on the corner of Victoria Rise, still administers to the soul.

Wandsworth Road in 1904, with horse-drawn tram car en route to East Hill, Wandsworth. The Portland Arms public house, 106 Wandsworth Road, stood on the corner of Pascal Street, later renamed Hamilton Street. Publican at the time was Mr Samuel Curtis. When the electric trams were introduced in 1909 the costermongers had to move their stalls into Wilcox Road opposite the pub.

Wandsworth Road near junction with Victoria Rise in 1910, with a small parade of shops supplying the everyday needs of locals. Note that vehicles are either horse-drawn or hand-pushed carts. This complete parade has been removed and four storey municipal housing has been erected on the site.

Mr Atkins stands proudly outside his shoe shop at 390 Wandsworth Road, at the corner of Thurlow Street, now called Pensbury Place, in 1906. A pair of workman's boots could be purchased for 4s 6d (22½p) or 5s 6d (27½p) and the most expensive shoes on display cost 11s 6d (57½p). The average weekly wage in 1914 for workers in the building industry was £2 0s 7d and in engineering £1 2s 10d.

Five

Clapham Buildings

Carlyle College, 83 West Side, Clapham Common, c. 1910. A private school for girls that taught music in preparation for Royal College of Music examinations and London matriculation. Boarders were taken in and a kindergarten department was in operation.

Manor House School, 58 North Side, Clapham Common, c. 1926, formerly known as The Beeches and before that as Byron House. The school was founded by Dr F.C. Maxwell, whose sons were to shine in the Arts, in 1876. Gorden Maxwell, a prolific writer who specialised in topographical works, mainly on London suburbs, was mentioned in despatches for his part in the Zeebrugge raid. Stanley Maxwell was headmaster of the school during the 1930's, whilst brother Donald illustrated Gorden's books, learning art at The Manor School and Clapham Art School. A plaque to forty-six "old boys" killed during the first world war is attached to the north wall of the parish church.

By 1926 the Montrose Hotel, with Mrs Shoneboom in charge, had absorbed Nos 64, 65, 66, 67 and 68 Southside, Clapham Common. No. 64 was previously named Pyne Lodge, No. 65 Fernwood House and No. 67 Henley Lodge, with a nursing home at No. 64 in 1913.

Clarence House in 1906 was in use by Battersea Polytechnic as a temporary secondary day school for girls while rebuilding was going on. A third floor balcony at the rear, known as Captain Cook's quarter deck when built, commanded a wonderful view to the Thames and beyond to Harrow on the Hill, but the explorer probably never lived at this address.

Clapham Public Library, c. 1908. An anonymous benefactor offered £2,000 towards the setting up of a public library in Clapham soon after Wandsworth's was opened in 1885. The library, built at a cost of £3,865, was opened by the Rt. Hon. Sir John Lubbock Bart, M.P. (later Lord Avebury) on 31st October 1889. The Ross Optical Co., established in New Bond Street in 1851 producing lenses for cameras and binoculars, moved here about 1892.

Doctor Barnado's Home, 49 High Street, Clapham, c. 1906. John Maillard was manager and general secretary of the Carter Home for boys. Doctor T. John Barnado (1845-1905), founder of the well-known homes for orphans, spent the last forty years of his life devoting himself to the protection and education of destitute children.

Clapham Fire Station, Orlando Road, Old Town, c. 1906. The L.C.C. ensured that modern local services were provided across the metropolis, and this station, built in 1902, superceded the old engine house (see page 17). Captain Thomas Ross, who laid out and developed Grafton Square in the 1840's and 1850's, lived at Cedar House, which had previously occupied the site. The present fire station was opened in 1964.

Salvation Army Citadel at the corner of Clapham Park Road and Park Hill, August 1908. The Edwardian era saw expansion in the work of the Salvation Army and they saw fit to open this new citadel on Saturday 8th August 1908.

17   CLAPHAM COMMON. — The Hostel. — LL.

Hostel of God, 29 North Side, Clapham Common, c. 1906. The Elms, built in 1754 for Thomas Page, a city businessman and stationer, was also the home of Sir Charles Barry, architect of many of our now famous buildings but best known for the present Houses of Parliament. The Free Home for the Dying, or Hostel of God, bought the house in 1899 and moved in the following year. Funding has enabled the hostel to acquire several neighbouring properties for the care of the terminally ill. Renamed the Trinity Hospice in 1980, they rely on 70 per cent of funding from donations and 30 per cent from local health authorities.

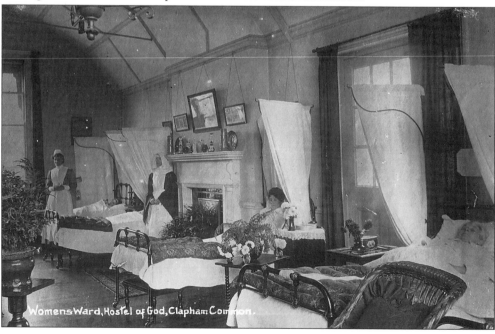

Womens Ward, Hostel of God, Clapham Common.

3660
CARD HOUSE.

Rectory Grove, c. 1910. The Bull's Head public house, now called The Fresian & Ferkin, with a recent delivery of ice from the horse and carts standing outside. The sacking was the only way to keep the ice from melting on the journey. The Rectory stood on this corner until it was demolished and the pub built in 1886. Amongst various incumbents was John Venn (hence Venn Street nearby) from 1792 until his death in July 1813, a much respected and popular vicar. The Rectory moved to Stowey House, a large building on Clapham Common, South Side, in 1856. The parochial school is to the left. The Old Manor House stood further down the Grove on the right.

High School for Girls, The Lawn, 63 Southside, Clapham Common, c. 1904. Just over 500 girls were administered by headmistress Miss A.S. Paul, who had been preceded by a Mrs Woodhouse .

South London Hospital for Women, South Side, Clapham Common, c. 1926. At this period 100 beds were available for women with an additional 25 beds for private patients. There was also an X-ray department and a recently added maternity ward for 25 patients. Queen Mary opened the hospital on 4th July 1916 with a steel key as part of the wartime economy drive. It was run and staffed entirely by females for the care of women and children and run on voluntary contributions. The hospital was enlarged in the 1930's but closed in 1984 and still lies empty ten years later.

Saint Mary's Catholic church, Clapham Park Road, c. 1930. Designed by William Wardell and built in 1851, the church was added to and enlarged over the years and a small monastery added. The spire, 172 ft high, is the last of three that stood in the area. The old City and South London station, sited here but demolished in 1930, is boarded up and awaiting development, but it was used as a ventilation shaft for a deep-level bomb shelter. The church bells were rung out for the first electric tram in May 1903, which took the Prince of Wales to Tooting, and also in November 1942 for the first wartime victory – El Alamein.

Woodlands, 24 Northside, Clapham Common, c. 1916, a guest house of the Co-operative Holidays Association in this photograph. Mrs J. Everett Hinchcliffe was secretary and manageress. The building was renamed Woodlands by railway engineer R.F. Fairlie when he moved to Clapham in 1862. The Tsar of Russia is rumoured to have been one of his guests here. The site is now occupied by a small block of flats erected during the 1930's which retains the name Woodlands.

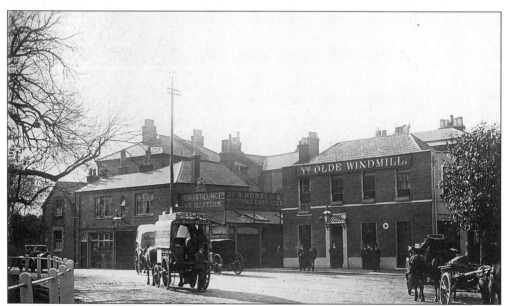

The Windmill public house, c. 1912. A public house has stood here since at least 1665. Two windmills stood nearby: one in Nightingale Lane and the other, probably a post-mill, on the common. Tilling & Son's operated the horse-drawn buses throughout London, but the stables here hired out carriages for weddings and the use of the large mansions by the common.

The High Street, c. 1910. The Electric Picture Palace cinema was down Venn Street, the hall of the auditorium looming up beyond The Plough. To aid public awareness the management had altered the first floor of A.I. Jones' tobacco shop and covered it with white stucco cherubs and ornamentation heralding their shows as "Topical, Refined and giving a Continuous Performance". The large passageway on the left of the Plough was the entrance to the horse-drawn tram depot, disused after 1903 when the electric service was introduced.

St Barnabas church, c. 1938, on the corner of North Side and Lavender Gardens. The foundation stone was laid in 1879 but the church was not consecrated until 1889. It stands in the grounds and in front of the Shrubbery, built in 1796 and extended in size by city merchant Alderman John Humphreys.

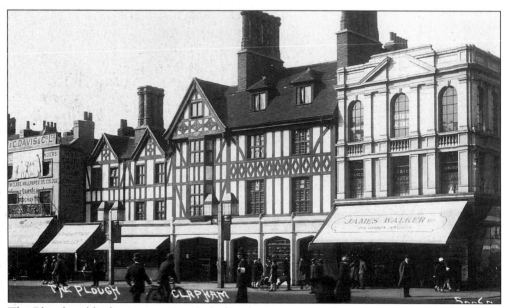

The Plough public house, c. 1928, recently rebuilt in the mock-tudor style, together with the jewellers shop on the corner. The cost of construction must have been high as even the chimneys copied the barley-sugar twist seen on Elizabethan houses.

Six
Clapham Common

Band Stand, Clapham Common.

The bandstand, c. 1910. Originally built as one of a pair in 1861 for the Royal Horticultural Society's garden in South Kensington and brought here in 1890, the bandstand was stripped of the cast iron balustrade during the last war and at some time lost the looped finial from the top. The second of the pair was taken to Peckham Rye park but no longer survives.

The Cockpond, summer of 1910, named after the Cock Tavern, a much altered public house that probably originated in the seventeenth century and can be seen in the gap in the trees below the church spire. The pinafores worn by the young girls was an original and bright way of keeping dresses and skirts clean on active children.

The Boating Pond, Southside, c. 1926. Eagle pond was made shallower between the wars, enabling children to go boating, but it is now just used for fishing.

The Sailing or Long Pond, Southside, c. 1912. Competition amongst modellers, whether steam, electric, diesel or sail, since the Victorian era, has ensured a continuous procession across the waves.

Sheep on the common, c. 1910. Frequently seen on the common before the last war, sheep were brought up from the country to feed on London's heaths and commons before travelling on to the markets. Railings to pen the sheep were removed for the war effort and postwar traffic prohibited their freedom to roam.

London Naval cadets practice with wooden rifles on the common along Southside, not far from Cavendish Road, in 1910. The Naval League was formed to ensure that Britons were aware of their naval heritage and to prepare and interest the young in maritime affairs.

Summertime, 1910 or 1911. Families relax after a stroll on the common, whilst two schoolgirls, carrying their books, find the time to pose for the photographer.

The Drinking Fountain, c. 1910. The bronze sculpture of a woman giving water to a beggar was commissioned by the United Kingdom Temperance & General Provident Institution from Frederick Muller of Munich in 1884, when the company was based in the City near London Bridge. The statue was brought to Clapham in 1894.

The tennis grounds on the common about 1910 has a look of gentle chaos about it, with members of the family and their dog resting in the middle of the court.

Hockey on the common, c. 1908. Inter-school rivalry amongst the many girls' schools surrounding the common must have made visiting this field rather exciting. How the young ladies managed to play in all their finery amazes the modern mind!

The Clapham Omnibus, c. 1912. A petrol-engined No. 37 bus passing by No. 13, North Side, known as Hollyhurst but now called Wren House. "The Man on the Clapham Omnibus" to describe a fair-minded, average man is supposed to have first been used by Lord Bowen, Master of the Rolls about 1875, but the Journal of the Society of Arts on 1st May 1857, referring to congestion in London, said, "Your occupant of the knife-board of a Clapham omnibus will stick on London Bridge for half-an-hour with scarcely a murmur".

West Side, Clapham Common, c. 1910. The large house seen through the trees is No. 85, now in use as the London Central Memorial Club for the Royal Antediluvian Order of Buffalos, a charitable organisation similar to the Masons. No. 84, to the left, is Western Lodge.

Long Road, Clapham Common, c. 1914, looking west towards Battersea from the roof of the Alexandra Hotel on Southside. The medieval name for Long Road and Northside was The Canterbury Way, mentioned in 1501. It is called Canterbury Road by 1718. Before the first world war races were held from The Plough to Battersea Rise with coalmen carrying a hundredweight (50kg) sack of coal.

Seven

Battersea
Clapham Junction

Arding & Hobbs department store in 1908. Built in 1885 as the largest department store south of the Thames, it could boast a telegram address of "Greatness" and a Battersea No. 4 telephone number. The store management and staff were expecting the usual bumper trading leading up to Christmas 1909 and the building was fully stocked and gaily decorated when, at approximately 4.20p.m. on 20th December, a disastrous fire broke out. The store and many surrounding buildings were soon a total wreck, with eight people losing their lives.

Fire at Arding & Hobbs, 20th December 1909. The tower of Francis & Sons, tailors in St John's Road, silhouetted against the inferno that had destroyed the major store by 6.30p.m. The fire was not under control until 9p.m. Estimated damage was put at £250,000. The band in the store played "I'm afraid to go home in the dark" while the store was evacuated, undertaken without any signs of panic.

GREAT FIRE AT ARDING AND HOBBS DEC 20 1909

The following morning saw crowds of photographers and curious onlookers milling about, incredulous at the scenes of devastation. The store had collapsed at the height of the blaze and piles of mangled steel and broken brick were all that was left to see. The five storey block in Ilminster Gardens was where 300 of the 600 staff lived and this too was a gutted shell. The view in St John's Road shows the pathetic remains of beds, previously on display, hanging from steel girders.

The following morning firemen were still playing their hoses on the smouldering ruins. Steel girders and rubble lie in St John's Road where they fell the previous evening. The 300 live-in staff lost all of their personal possessions and were, of course, made homeless, temporary accommodation being provided the following night. Harrods, Gorringes and many other stores swiftly offered donations, which amounted to £6,000 by the 26th December.

Francis & Son's, men's outfitters across St John's Road from Arding & Hobbs, had displayed a variety of chickens and turkeys for Christmas sale. This store was badly damaged, and in the blaze the birds were prematurely cooked! Windows were cracked in the Falcon public house on the far corner, some 30 to 40 yards away.

Arding & Hobbs, c. 1917. The site of the old store was cleared, adjoining properties bought up, architects drawings and specifications made out, men and materials gathered together, and in a stupendous effort the new store was open for business on 5th December 1910. One workman was killed on 5th May 1910 when the jib of a crane broke and he fell nearly 100 ft. The store is thought of as the central point of Clapham Junction and directions are often given mentioning the name. The canvas blinds have been replaced with a permanent canopy over the pavement.

St John's Hill, c. 1926. Arding & Hobbs' store towers above Lavender Hill. With very little private traffic on the streets trams and buses were kings of the road. Less space was taken up by the L.C.C. tram, which was only 7ft wide (the modern bus is 8ft. 2½in). The Imperial cinema, renamed The Ruby, was demolished, together with the bank alongside, during the 1980's.

Clapham Junction Station, c. 1912. The high level entrance was enlarged in 1910 by the London Brighton and South Coast Railway. The parcels entrance in St John's Hill has been closed for many years but is presently undergoing stone cleaning. A complex system of railway lines pass through Battersea and when Falcon Junction was rebuilt as a passenger station, in 1863, the name Clapham Junction was given rather than the more correct Battersea Junction.

Clapham Junction, c. 1928. St John's Hill is at the centre, with Battersea Grammar school at the corner of Plough Road where The Granada cinema was later built. St Mark's church, on the triangle to the right, and the Masonic girls' school, in the centre, were replaced by a housing estate in the 1930's. The many lines of the station and the Plough Road sidings occupy several acres of land. St John's Road and the noticeable curve of Lavender Sweep lie beyond the block of Arding & Hobbs.

Clapham Junction, c. 1928. Plough Road school and the Victorian Plough public house are at centre, with St John's Hill running from right to left. Battersea Rise and the site of New Wandsworth station and coal depot, closed in 1968, are far right. Northcote Road is to the top of the picture.

St John's Hill in 1907. The Surrey Hounds public house, on the corner of Plough Terrace, was involved in a disastrous incident on 17th June 1944, when a V1 flying bomb virtually destroyed the pub and neighbouring shops, causing many casualties here and in two passing buses.

St John's Hill in 1907. St Paul's church, consecrated in 1868, was designed by a Mr Coe and cost £6,300 to build. St John's was the family name of the Lords of the Manor of Battersea, who held the title from 1627 to 1763 when the Spencer family gained the estate.

Thanks to Mr Powell's sweetshop and newsagents, in St John's Hill, with the news hoarding proclaiming the 50th anniversary of the Indian Mutiny, we know the date of this view to be 1907. To confirm this, Benjamin & Co. have a new wallpaper catalogue for 1907 in the window. Next to Mr Page's hairdressing saloon, which charged 3d for haircutting or 2½d for a shave, is The Prince of Wales public house.

Vardens Road, c. 1912. The snooker hall at the far end of the road was originally built as a roller skating rink and taken over by Mulliners in 1910 to repair aeroplanes. Mrs Hilda Hewlett, with Gustav Blondeau, opened an aeroplane factory in the building in 1912, which moved to larger premises in Bedford in 1914. Mrs Hewlett, who was the first woman to gain an aviators licence, No. 122, lived at 34 Park Mansions, Prince of Wales Road, opposite Battersea Park.

St John's Road is the major shopping street of the district and has changed little since this view of 1912, except for the loss of family owned enterprises. Farrows bank, on the left, promoted itself as "the people's bank", but when it foundered in the 1920's many local people lost their savings and deposits.

Battersea Rise, c. 1912. This popular parade of shops has included over the years almost every supplier imaginable: bakers, off-licence, tobacconists, furniture showroom, grocers, and restaurant. In Edwardian times children going to the Oil shop for their parents would often be given a poke of sweets (a newspaper funnel) for their custom, and when bakers weighed out bread the makeweight was often a small bun rapidly eaten on the way home.

Northcote Road, c. 1910. The costermongers' stalls were illegally set up in the 1880's and many fights ensued with shopkeepers in St John's Road and Battersea Rise. Those in Northcote Road were eventually sanctioned and still provide a variety of produce from their hand-pushed carts. Excitement was to be had in earlier times waiting for bargains as midnight approached on Christmas Eve.

Mr H. Acland's shop, 74 Northcote Road, seen here in 1907, produced a series of postcard views of local street scenes that are now much sought after. Mr Acland's shop sold stationery and fancy paper goods and was also a sub post office.

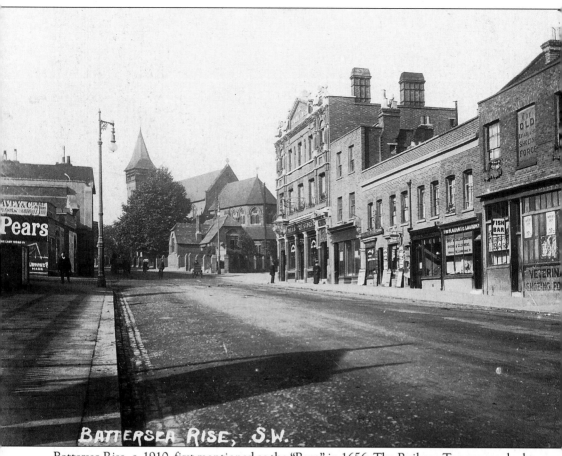

Battersea Rise, c. 1910, first mentioned as the "Ryse" in 1656. The Railway Tavern, no doubt so called for it's proximity to the New Wandsworth railway station on the common, has been renamed The Dog and Duck. Sign of the times is the Old Shoeing Forge of Harvey & Evans, closed and "To Let". Many a child stopping to warm themselves during the winter has stood bewitched by the men hitting the white-hot iron to make the shoes. St Mark's church, designed by Mr William White, was built in 1873 at a cost of £6,500 and consecrated on 30th September 1874.

Lavender Hill in 1910, with a delivery cart for Nevills bread, at 2d a loaf, struggling up the incline past the parade of shops on the right which was destroyed during the second world war. The foundation stone for the library was laid by Sir John Lubbock on 2nd May 1889. Costing £8,600 to construct, it was opened on 26th March 1890 by Mr A.J. Mundella, M.P.

Clapham Junction Post Office, Lavender Hill, c. 1910. Progress over the years alters many things but the opening hours in 1910 were "For the sale of stamps 8a.m. to 10p.m. and for other business 10a.m. to 8p.m. Sundays 9a.m.-10a.m. and 5p.m.-6p.m. with a general collection at 12.30 midnight". The building was opened in 1898 and rebuilt in 1961.

Lavender Hill, c. 1910. The South Western Magistrates Court and Police Station on the left were rebuilt as a single unit in 1963.

Lavender Hill junction with Sugden Road, c. 1910. Ninety years previously, in 1820, William Pamplin, a noted florist, had his nurseries and planting grounds on Lavender Hill. Lavender was grown commercially by the acre for use in perfume manufacture.

Queens Road, c. 1930, renamed Queenstown Road in 1939 to avoid confusion with the many other Queens Roads in London. Francis Manns' store later became Hemmings bakers, and in September 1950 was totally demolished by a runaway tram unable to make the left turn from Cedars Road. The store on the right was lost to wartime bombing and has never been rebuilt.

Queens Road, c. 1910. Young boys stand by the Wesleyan Methodist church and school room, on the corner of Stanley Street, whose foundation stone was laid 15th July 1881. The single deck trams were in use until the rail bridges further along the road were altered in 1927 to take double deckers. The road was laid out in 1863 as the main spine of the Park Town estate development in which J.T. Knowles was employed.

S.Philip's Church, Queen's Road.   S.S. Series. 7100.

Local landowner Mr Philip W. Flower donated the site, and the new churh of St Philip, Queenstown Road, costing £13,000 and seen here in 1910, was dedicated by Bishop Wilberforce in 1870. Built to house almost a thousand worshippers the original proposal was to include a lofty spire and flying buttresses resulting in a most imposing structure.

POST OFFICE   QUEENS RD   BATTERSEA

Queenstown Road, c. 1919. The sub post office at No. 109 was run by Misses Grace and Daisy Clark. Shops were provided only at the northern end of the road at the outset of development in 1863, and this row and others nearer the Wandsworth Road had to be built out beyond the frontage planned.

Eight

Battersea Old Town

St Mary's parish church, Battersea, c. 1910. The church dates from November 1777 and took two years to build. The original scheme in 1776 was to paint the copper of the spire a stone colour but this was deferred due to the oncoming winter; the pleasing green was deemed sufficient and it is the colour we enjoy today. There are monuments to Lord Grandison (1630), Viscount and Lady Bolingbroke (1751 and 1749) and many others, including the stained glass window to Benedict Arnold of the American War of Independence .

Battersea High Street, c. 1912, viewed from Falcon Road. This end of the High Street was only developed in the 1880's; before that it was just a small lane leading out from the village to the London Road, with only a stagnant pond and the town gates. The Princes Head public house nearby was still a small country wayside inn. The clatter and noise of carts on cobblestone roads, the street cries of catsmeat men, hokey-pokey ice-cream sellers, organ grinders and the shouts of costermongers must have made the streets a lively sea of humanity.

Opposite: Battersea Square, c. 1915. Prior to the 1860's this was the hub of the commercial life of the village, with the best shops and the many trades allied to work on the land and nearby river, by which most passengers and merchandise would arrive or leave. Although well known as Battersea Square, it is in fact a triangle and does not appear as an address. The numbering system is for the High Street or Vicarage Crescent.

Southlands College, High Street, c. 1910, built for the Duchess of Angouleme during the French Revolution and known as "The Retreat". Field Marshall Sir George Pollock changed the name to Southlands when he moved here in 1840. From 1870 until 1926 the house was in use as a Wesleyan teacher training college. Almost completely destroyed by bombing in the second world war, the ruins were used by civil defence forces. The taller building was to become Southlands public library. The two urns on the entrance were made from an artificial stone produced by Coade of Lambeth at the end of the eighteenth century. Their secret is lost but the stone does not corrode.

High Street, c. 1910. The Woodman public house on the right is the older of the pubs, the other called, confusingly, The Original Woodman, is younger. Green and London, ironmongers at No. 77, proudly named their shop The Surrey Ironworks. Albert Simmons had the Oilman and Hardware shop, while beyond Trott Street was an eel and pie shop with, next, Mrs Duffin, a catsmeat purveyor. Beyond the eighteenth-century cottages stands The Castle public house, an inn dating from the seventeenth century that was demolished in 1963 and rebuilt in 1964.

Battersea Bridge Road, c. 1910. The tram is en route to Beaufort Street terminus in Chelsea. The police station was here by 1884 and The Union Arms public house, on the right, probably dates from the same time. Vast postwar municipal development has demolished the majority of these dwellings.

Battersea Bridge Road, c. 1910, at the junction with Westbridge Road. The Prodigal's Return public house is on the left and the Earl Spencer public house further down on the right. A notice on the lamp post informs us that electricity supplied by Battersea Council from their Lombard Road power station cost $3\frac{1}{2}$d per unit. The road is first mentioned in 1598, when the surveyor for the parish was paid 5 shillings by "Willm Prichard the ferrie-man for the bringing of gravell to amend the fferie lane."

Battersea Bridge, c. 1910. The L.C.C. fire brigade station, besides a compliment of road vehicles, also had facilities for fire floats on the river nearby. A small tramway depot was incorporated alongside for the supply of sand to the tram shed depots, the trams having sand chutes that trickled small amounts on the rails to stop wheels slipping in spring and winter.

Park Road, at the junction of Radstock Street, c. 1912, remamed Parkgate Road by the L.C.C., no doubt on account of the park gates seen in the distance. Industrial concerns included J.B. Stevenson, bakeries, the Texas Oil Co., Thomas Lloyd Dairy Co. and, up until recent times, United Carlo Gatti, ice manufacturers.

Albert Bridge, c. 1920. Designed by a Mr Page and costing £88,000 to construct, the bridge was opened in 1857. A notice appears at either end to the effect that marching troops must break step or the oscillations would bring the bridge down. A central support has had to be added because of the wear of modern traffic.

Chelsea Bridge, c. 1914. Originally called Victoria Bridge to complement the Albert Bridge upstream, it was opened for traffic on 28th March 1858 and the tolls were abolished on 24th May 1879. The old bridge was removed in 1935 and reopened as Chelsea Bridge on 6th May 1937.

Battersea Park Road, c. 1912, at the junction with Falcon Road. Hunt and Cole's drapery store doesn't appear to have a square inch of space left in their window display. The dining rooms were run by a Mr John Spain. W.J. Harris & Co., perambulator manufacturers founded in 1912, sold their products on easy terms. Mr John George Bull was proprietor of the newsagents.

Battersea Park Road, c. 1910. The General Havelock public house, on the corner of Austin Road, was named after the hero of the Indian Mutiny. Following on is The Cricketeers public house. Henry Smith & Sons, funeral directors, had a fleet of Armstrong Siddeley cars and liveried chauffeurs for hire during the 1930's. Many side roads, such as Doddington Grove, Kilton Street, Park Grove and Landseer Street, have disappeared under housing.

Spiers and Pond Laundry, 140 Battersea Park Road, c. 1909. The laundry was erected in 1879 and this large firm cleaned linen for most of the larger hotels and establishments in the West End. Many hundreds of local women were able to supplement their family income either by taking in washing or with employment at these laundries.

London and Provincial Laundry, 154 Battersea Park Road, c. 1914. Opened about 1880, the works of $1\frac{1}{2}$ acres employed 150 staff, of whom 32 lived on the premises. Weekly turnover of 90,000 items required many stages of operation besides washing and drying, starching and ironing, such as the essentials of sorting and labelling. The vehicle is evidently new and the photograph taken for advertising purposes. The company was later renamed the Marie Blanche Laundry.

Battersea Park Road, c. 1910. The Cricketeers public house, which provided billiards and snooker rooms, also served "Hot luncheons for their patrons". Mr W. Parry's vegetable and fruit shop had a caged bird to amuse young children. Fun and games were also the result of cattle and sheep being driven along this road into nearby Chesney Street where the slaughterhouse stood.

Battersea Park Road at the junction with Queenstown Road, c. 1926. Checkley's newsagents and post office, on the right, continues to operate, although under a different management. With the increase in ownership of cars, the policemen had to go on point duty, directing traffic at busy junctions before the introduction of automatic signals in the 1930's. Everything on the left has disappeared under modern blocks of flats.

Nine

Battersea
Buildings and People

Battersea Power Station, c. 1935. The collier *John Hoplinson* of the London Power Company is adding to the 85,000 ton stockpile of coal held for use in this cathedral of power. Work started on the "A" station in 1929 and was completed in 1935, with the original pair of chimneys in use by 1933. The second, or "B" station, commissioned in 1944, was completed in 1955, by which time 875 people were employed at Battersea. The power station closed in 1983, and plans to convert it into a leisure complex have foundered. The structure remains (in 1994) an empty shell.

The Prince's Head public house, c. 1914. This pub, which stood on the corner of Falcon Road and York Road, was often given as the destination on a bus, tram or trolleybus. The Prince of Wales' bust, on the York Road frontage, disappeared during demolition in 1977. Captain Windham, whose motor body works at 20a to 26a StJohn's Hill was heavily engaged in building aeroplanes and overflowing with work, had his own aeroplane of bamboo constructed on the roof of the pub in 1909, but when taken to Wembley the aircraft was unsuccessful.

Town Hall, Lavender Hill, c. 1910. Opened in 1893 by Lord Rosebury, the Town Hall also had concert halls where dancing and cinema shows were held. When Battersea was merged with the borough of Wandsworth in 1965 the building became redundant but has now found a role as the Battersea Arts Centre. The Shakespeare Theatre, alongside, with 1,205 seats, opened in 1896 for dramatic performances but also staged Christmas pantomimes. By 1912 permission was sought from the council for cinema performances and it was fully converted for that in 1923. Badly damaged in 1940 by fire bombs, it was demolished in January 1957.

Pavilion Cinema, Lavender Hill, c. 1920. Mr Sydney Lyndon, who transferred from managing the Putney Pavilion, was manager on opening in 1916, the entertainment including an organ and orchestra. The building suffered from a V1 doodlebug on 17th August 1944, when 14 people in a passing No. 77 bus were killed as well as a further 14 persons on the streets and in nearby buildings. The site remained empty for forty years until the construction of a supermarket.

The Grand Music Hall, St John's Hill, c. 1904. The music hall artist Dan Leno invested heavily in the construction, which started with the foundation stone laying in May 1899, and a plaque (now in Wandsworth Museum) was unveiled at the opening in 1900. Later it became the Essoldo cinema and the Essoldo bingo club. Empty for a while, the Grand has been refurbished and reopened as a rock concert venue. Marie Lloyd, Little Titch, Harry Tate (who lived in Tooting) and even a troop of elephants, have appeared on the (specially strengthened) stage.

The Granada, St John's Hill, shortly after opening in November 1937. It occupies the site of the grammar school which moved to Streatham in 1936. The stop press notice board at the entrance announces "News reel pictures of submarine disaster". The last film was shown in 1979 and the building renamed and reused as The Gala Bingo Club.

The Antivivisection Hospital, seen here about 1908, stood on the corner of Albert Bridge Road and Prince of Wales Road. Formerly a private residence, it was converted to a hospital in 1902, largely due to the generosity of Elizabeth, Lady Headley, a firm protagonist of saving animals from medical experiments. Also known as Battersea General, the hospital, commonly called the "Viv" or the "AntiViv", was demolished in 1971. Members of The Haberdashers Cycling Club helped to gather funds, in about 1910, with a large model of the army airship *Nulli Secundis*. Annual parades near Easter were held as fund raising events.

Mr Alfred Reuter stands proudly in the entrance of his men's hairdressing saloon, at 182 Battersea Park Road, where a profusion of men's toiletries and dress accessories are displayed, in 1907. A common method of sharing rents and rates was to let half a shop and the other half was taken up by Mr E. Kemp, who recovered and repaired umbrellas.

Mr George Russell Pulford, who lived at 183 Battersea Bridge Road, with his horse-drawn coffee and tea stalls outside the gates of Battersea Park at Queens Circus, about 1914. In the background is All Saints' church, consecrated in 1883, damaged by fire in 1969 and demolished soon after.

The Rising Sun public house, 186 Battersea Bridge Road, on the corner of Surrey Lane, in about 1922. Mr William Glover was the publican in 1902.

The Plough public house, St John's Hill, c. 1907. First mentioned in 1681, the pub was on an important route from Kingston to London. The earlier building was demolished and rebuilt in 1875 by Young & Co., the Wandsworth brewers. This building was destroyed by bombing in 1940 and not replaced until 1958.

Bolingbroke Hospital, Bolingbroke Grove, c. 1910, originally one of five houses built in the early part of the nineteenth century and called Bolingbroke House. Canon Clarke instigated the purchase and alterations at a cost of £6,000, enabling the first patient to be admitted in 1880 to "The Bolingbroke Self-Supporting Hospital and House in Sickness". The house was demolished in the 1930's for extensions to the hospital.

George Lodge & Sons, 73 Northcote Road. In 1910 they were trading as corn chandlers, but they are also listed as trading in 1902 from 91 St Ann's Hill, Wandsworth. The Northcote address had become a confectioners by 1917, most of London's horses having by this time been taken to France so that Mr Lodge probably had few patrons.

The Northcote Hotel, Northcote Road, c. 1930. At the time of development in the 1860's there were just a few cottages and Bolingbroke farm here. In 1773 the fields were covered in wheat, potatoes and barley, and the Falcon brook was an open ditch or sewer with a small wooden bridge at the crossroads of Northcote Road and Battersea Rise. The Metropolitan Board of Works approved in January 1865 the expenditure of £30,000 to cover in, deepen and redirect the length of the Falcon brook from Balham to the Thames.

Mr George James Barber in 1907, with the staff of his farriers shop at 179a Church Road, Battersea. Many farriers went out of business during the first world war because of the requisitioning of horses for the western front. Children were sometimes allowed to operate the bellows but were horrified at the clouds of smoke given off when the shoes were placed on the hooves, little realising no harm was done.

The 7th Battersea wolf cubs, c. 1919. The first scout troop in Battersea was formed in 1909 and very quickly expanded to the extent that the 7th was formed at St George's, Nine Elms in April 1910 by the Rev. E. Wilson Hill. It soon had 200 members. Cub scouts were allowed in 1916 and the boys were soon cycling round the streets with bugles sounding the "Take Cover" or "All Clear" before and after air raids.

Clapham Junction, c. 1904. *Rastrick*, a class B2 locomotive built in 1896 by the London Brighton & South Coast Railway, shown here in the original "Improved Green" livery (actually an orange-yellow shade), was repainted dark green in 1905, rebuilt in 1910 and finally withdrawn in 1930.

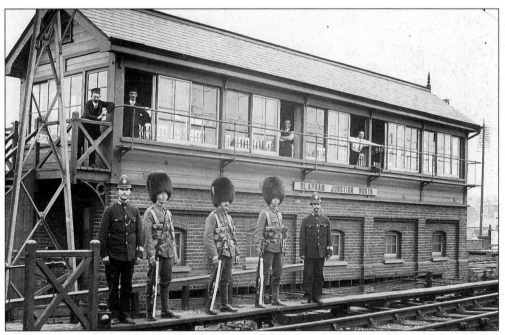

Clapham Junction North signal box during the railway strike of 1911. A series of labour disputes in the docks and coalmines, that had led to injuries and even deaths, convinced the goverment of the need to protect vital facilities. The troops and police were detailed to guard all the signal boxes and other places for the safety of those continuing to work. The railway strike started on 13th August and all went back to work on 21st August.

Battersea Bridge, c. 1910. The old wooden bridge, drawn and painted by many artists including Turner and Whistler, replaced the ancient ferry to *Chelchehith*. The ferry, owned by the crown, was sold by James I to the Earl of Lincoln for £40 in 1603. The bridge was closed in November 1885 and the Earl of Rosebury, 1st Chairman of the L.C.C., opened the present bridge, designed by Sir Joseph and Mr Edward Bazalgette and costing £143,000, on 21st July 1890.

Lord John Sanger's travelling circus in September 1928. Mr Arthur Moule, with the cane, was bandmaster in charge until 1935. The circus appeared locally at The Grand, Clapham Junction, and yearly on Clapham Common.

The Falcon public house, c. 1907, on the corner of Falcon Road and St John's Hill, was rebuilt in the 1880's to replace an earlier pub which had the Falcon brook running outside, a horse trough and was surrounded by orchards and floral gardens. The earliest reference is in 1767, when £9 5s was given to Mrs Smith at the "Faulcon" for what was then an expensive dinner for the churchwardens of St Mary's parish. In about 1800 the publican's name was Robert Death and funeral parties would stop at the Falcon to slake their thirsts. These occasions would often turn into scenes of merriment. The artist John Nixon happened upon such a scene and sketched the celebrants, which was soon published, of the undertakers at "Deaths Door".

Church of St Vincent de Paul, Altenburg Gardens, c. 1907. The Catholic community had purchased No. 5 (renumbered No. 36.) for use as a chapel and centre for local worshippers. Attached was a small orchard deemed suitable for a church and the foundation stone was laid on Saturday 28th July 1906 with the Bishop of Southwark in attendance. The church was opened on Tuesday 19th March 1907 by the Bishop of Nottingham, Monsignor Robert Brindle.

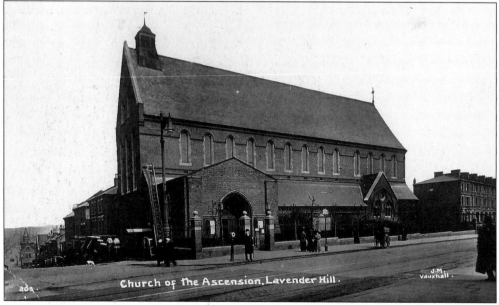

Church of the Ascension, Lavender Hill, c. 1910. The foundation stone was laid on 1st June 1876 by the Earl of Glasgow but the church took until 1893 to complete. The lantern on the roof was destroyed by fire in the 1970's. The address of the church in local directories of the time also included the fire escape ladder kept to the left of the entrance. Rails for the sliding gates enclosing the escape are still (1994) in evidence.

St George's church, Nine Elms Lane, c. 1910. Edward Blore was the architect of this early Gothic Revival building of brick construction, consecrated in 1829 and costing just over £2,900. It was known as St George's in the Fields, for at that time the railways had not arrived and only fields and waterside mills existed. The fields were soon covered by industry, railways (after 1838), and Chelsea waterworks reservoirs (where the power station was built), and by 1858 Nine Elms gasworks occupied seventeen acres.

Nine Elms Station (c. 1910) opened in 1838 as the London terminus of the London and South Western Railway Co. Soon bypassed by the opening of Waterloo in 1848, Nine Elms was left as just a goods station. Rail lines crossing Nine Elms Lane to riverside wharfs had also to cross over tram lines, and a man with a flag had to accompany wagons over the road. The station was demolished in 1968.

St John's College, High Street, c. 1910, founded in 1700 with a charitable bequest by Sir Walter St John, lord of the manor, for twenty scholars, together with a house and garden. The school was rebuilt in 1859 and again in 1913-14, with extensions since. The grammar school on St John's Hill was added in 1875. Two large stained glass windows in memory of seventy-seven old boys killed in the first world war were unveiled by Earl Haig in 1921. Senior students and masters are seen, below, outside the extension built onto the rear of Battersea House, which dates from 1699 and survives.

Ten
Battersea Streets

Battersea Square (c. 1907) originally known as the "Elme Trees" (in 1656), is where the stocks and watchhouse stood. The elms, originally surrounded by rails, survived until 1925, when the last tree was noted as being "dead, killed off by the tar paving that surrounds it". The Square was renamed as early as 1793. A village pump replaced the stocks in 1811, at a cost of £ 47 1s 6d, but was removed in 1873. The stocks were moved to St Mary's church and last used in 1821.

Prince of Wales Drive, c. 1910. The mansions were built on land set aside when Battersea Park was laid out. The Albert Palace, a similar design to the Crystal Palace, was built in 1882-3 and occupied ten acres in the general area of Lurline Gardens. The company was unsuccessful and the venture closed in 1888, demolition occurring in 1893. Albert Palace mansions and Prince of Wales mansions occupy the site of the building; Battersea Polytechnic and York mansions cover the site of the Albert's gardens and terraces.

Bolingbroke Grove, c. 1909. Known as Five Houses Lane up until the British Land Co. commenced development in 1858, the road skirted Battersea west common, now renamed Wandsworth Common. Named after a descendant of Sir Oliver St John, Viscount Grandison, who in 1712 became Viscount Bolingbroke, the road was originally laid out before 1828 by a Mr Bush and Mr Perkins of East Hill, Wandsworth.

No. 33 Tyneham Road, c. 1926. Robert Marriott, registered as a beer retailer, is seen with a recent delivery from Hammertons of Stockwell in the roadway. He also has an excellent display of wines in the shop window.

David Thomas, Falcon Road, c. 1912. The firm sold a selection of millinery and household drapery, together with a range of dolls and toys. The whole block was taken over by them in their expansion. An eye-catching sign above the store appears blurred at first sight but was like that only to attract attention.

Baptist chapel, Northcote Road, c. 1919. A No. 49a is passing the chapel designed by the local architect Mr E.W. Mountford. Completed during 1889, the building has not been altered much.

Vicarage Gardens, c. 1910. This small park adjacent to the Thames was an unusual oasis amid the mills and factories of Battersea. It was given to the parish to use when Battersea House became part of St John's school.

Webbs Road, c. 1907. The Webb family owned a considerable portion of land adjacent to Clapham Common, developed from 1880 onwards. Webbs Lane or Popes Road, as it was called, was unpaved up to this date and wandering animals from local piggeries were causing some nuisance to residents in Chatham Road and Battersea Rise.

Tennyson Street, c. 1915. The Poet Laureate, Lord Alfred Tennyson, had in 1871 bought up the freehold of twenty-seven houses at the northern end of the Park Town development as an investment, but had disposed of them by 1882. Nearby streets are named after British authors – Dickens Street, Thackery Street, Ruskin Street and Trollope Street – but also honoured is Gambetta, the French statesman who gained prominence during the seige of Paris, 1870-1.

Mallinson Road, c. 1910. Approved by Battersea vestry in 1869, the road by 1878 only had forty-four properties occupied, but two years later eighty had been taken up. The Methodist chapel nearer the Bolingbroke Grove was opened 9th July 1887. An unusual feature of roads in south Battersea is the splitting into three sections of four roads by Northcote Road and Webbs Road.

Louvaine Road, c. 1907. A small school called the Louvaine Academy was in operation at No. 16 in the years 1865 to 1875. Three storey development in this area is unususal but was no doubt encouraged by the opening in 1863 of the nearby Clapham Junction railway station.

Wroughton Road, c. 1910. As part of the general expansion of south Battersea, the road was approved in July 1880 as part of the Broomwood Park Estate building plan, together with six nearby roads that were not fully available until the 1890's. The trees were probably a relic of the field boundaries surviving from the days before the bricks and mortar arrived.

Hillier Road, c. 1910. William Thomas Bray, resident here in the 1890's, was a poor law administrator for the Wandsworth and Clapham Union and had, with other committee members, a ward at the hospital for the aged poor at Church Lane, Tooting, named after him. The Guardians bought the hospital (which later became St Benedict's) in 1895.

Elspeth Road, c. 1910. Construction of houses had reached No. 17. by 1891. To judge from their size the trees must have been planted by the turn of the century but have not survived, the road becoming too narrow for modern traffic to cope with the spreading foliage.

Grandison Road, c. 1910. Lords of the manor of Battersea from 1627 to 1763, the St John family had as part of their name the title Viscount Grandison, which stems from the fifteenth century, when Oliver St John married Lady Margaret Beauchamp from Wiltshire, whose descent was traced through William de Grandison (died 1335).

Broomwood Road, c. 1910. William Wilberforce died in 1833, having just heard that the bill for the emancipation of slaves had been passed by the Houses of Parliament. Broomfield, the house where he lived and died, stood behind No. 111 Broomwood Road, where the mayor of Wandsworth Council, E.S. Strange, laid a wreath on 4th July 1933 to commemorate Wilberforce's death. The great man was buried in Westminster Abbey and a statue to his memory was erected there.

Salcott Road, c. 1907. When the road was laid in 1869 the area was still much in agricultural use, and in 1874 the few residents were complaining of the proximity of goats to their properties. The fields were quickly swallowed up: by 1878, thirty-nine houses were completed and sixty-one by 1880.

Sabine Road, c. 1907. The Shaftesbury Park Estate, formerly part of Poupart's market gardens, was laid out by the Artisans, Labourers and General Dwelling Co. and the first stone was laid by the Earl of Shaftesbury in 1872. The scheme involved erecting 1,100 houses from which taverns and beer houses were excluded.

Lavender Gardens, c. 1910. A bakery delivery boy with a large wicker basket slung over his shoulders stands grinning at the camera. A school leaving age of 14 years ensured a steady supply of delivery boys for work in the many local shops, which, in the absence of means of keeping food fresh, had to offer a daily service.

Sugden Road, c. 1910. The church of the Ascension, Lavender Hill, stands proudly at the far end of the road. Development started in this road in 1877. The cast iron railings were requisitioned and removed during the second world war for use in munitions production. Those that survive in Battersea are on buildings with basements or where safety was a special consideration.

Belleville Road, c. 1910. The valley formed by the Falcon brook is well pronounced in this view, with Belleville Road school and Webbs Road in the far distance. As part of the Conservative Land Societies estate development, the eastern arm of the road was given approval in 1875, and by 1880 residents had moved into fifty-one of the new properties.

Cambridge Road, c. 1912, part of the development of the Battersea fields left over after the formation of Battersea park. It is interesting to note that Cambridge Road in Putney was renamed (it is now Werter Road) by the L.C.C. to forestall any confusion of place names in the south west of London.

Battersea Park Road, c. 1908. Christchurch, dedicated by the Bishop of Winchester on 27th July 1849, cost £5,586 to construct and was designed by a Mr Talbot Bury. The church was destroyed by a V2 rocket on a Sunday in November 1944, and the church gardens, laid out for public use in 1884, were rededicated to Battersea's war dead after the second world war. The tall tower of the fire station, on the left, was destroyed in the same incident.The town gate and pound stood here to stop animals wandering among the crops.

Eleven

Battersea Park

Battersea park lake, c. 1910. Formed from the old marshes and market gardens, the park had a millon cubic yards of earth brought here from excavation of the London Docks to raise the levels. At a cost of £312,000, 200 acres of parkland was opened on 28th March 1858 and a further 120 acres sold off to defray the costs.

The Sub-Tropical Gardens in 1912 was one of many well-manicured attractions to educate and amuse the visitor. Mulberry, Indian Rubber and Vanilla trees, date and palm, bamboo, banana and pampas were amongst a few of the exotic plants nurtured here. The small railings to separate grass and visitor were removed during the second world war.

The greenhouse display in 1908 of chrysanthemums and exotic plants ready for the annual show held in the conservatories about the middle of October each year.

Cricket nets, c. 1908. Provision for sports and recreation within the park has been excellent from day one. The Battersea Cricket Club, formed in 1856, had its headquarters in The Prince Albert public house and used the park for matches.

The Japanese garden, c. 1910, a popular attraction, with wooden pagoda-like structures containing miniature bonsai trees and other Asian exotics.

The aviary, c. 1906. Several varieties of pigeon, fantails, tumblers, dun dragons, red jacobins, pouters and rollers were kept together with a raven and common and golden pheasants. A smaller aviary nearby held the following birds: goldfinch, bullfinch, chaffinch, bramblefinch, linnet and twite. Peacocks, turkeys and owls were also looked after.

The boating lake, c. 1910. Fifteen acres of water given over for the pleasure of boating is shared with geese, ducks, moorhens and swans. Fish life included roach, bream, tench, eel and carp.

The bandstand, c. 1912. Listening to band concerts prior to the first world war was a popular way of spending Sundays and holiday weekends. The park was often used for political meetings, and during the second world war the bandstand was a convenient platform for speeches in aid of the Soviet Union.

The attentive audience at the bandstand in 1905 is listening to a demonstration of the Auxeto-gramophone, invented by Horace Short, whose brothers had a balloon factory in railway arches at Queens Circus to the east of the park. The Auxeto-gramophone, demonstrated at the 1900 Paris exhibition, used compressed air to project the sound at pressure from the megaphone.

The English garden, c. 1912, a recently introduced feature to the park with lupins, roses and several trellis-trained varieties. The small pond, with a small fountain on top of the urn, contained goldfish and water lilies. Queen Mary would often visit the park and considered Battersea to be of the best London parks.

Deer in the park, c. 1912. Approximately half a dozen fallow deer were kept in the hilly enclosure towards the eastern end of the park.

The war memorial is to commemorate the XXIV Division London Regiment which served in France, 1914-18. The unveiling was carried out by Field Marshall Lord Plummer on Saturday 4th October 1924. Mr Eric Kennington was the sculptor.

The Festival of Britain in 1951 was held to commemorate the 1851 Great Exhibition and to assist Britain in coming out of wartime drudgery. Bedevilled by strikes of electricians and carpenters, and the opposition of regular users of the park and occupants of the mansions nearby, the pleasure gardens opened in May 1951.

An additional attraction for 1951 was the funfair, left in operation with a few alterations to the rides until 1974. In this scene is Max Myer's Rotor and Makin's Hurricane. Other rides were the caterpillar, dodgems, waltzer, gallopers and roundabouts. The showman John Collins brought his Big Dipper ride by road from Sutton Coldfield, hauled by two steam traction engines, in November 1950. The fairground was closed on Sundays during 1951.

THE AMPHITHEATRE, BATTERSEA GARDENS, LONDON.

The amphitheatre, erected in 1951, had a capacity of 2,000 (1,300 seated) for outdoor performances of ballet and the appearances of bands. Divine services were held at 3p.m. under a committee of combined Battersea churches. Every night the stage became the Lambeth Arms, where cockney characters, under the direction of Leonard Sachs, would deliver the Lambeth Walk, etc.

Eagerly awaited by visitors was the striking of the hour of the Guinness clock, when the animated mechanism started in motion: the mad hatter attempting to catch fish, an ostrich emerging, a spinning sun, toucans pecking at a tree and the guinness zoo-keeper appearing from under an umbrella were a few of the movements.

The 1951 boating lake, with the funfair at the far side, had underwater lighting, which gave a pale blue hue at night, a small lighthouse on an island, and surrounding custom house, chapel, net loft and ship's chandlers. The Field gasholder, erected by a German company in the 1930's, looms up beyond the park.

Rowland Emmett, well-known in the pages of *Punch*, designed the engines and equipment for the Far Tottering and Oystercreek railway. The little diesel engines, *Nellie*, *Neptune* and *Wildgoose*, transported 1,000 passengers per hour around the grounds. An unfortunate head-on collision involving *Nellie* and *Wildgoose* on 11th July 1951 resulted in the death of a woman passenger.

The tree walk, sponsored by Franco Signs, went as high as 30 feet amongst the branches. A village in the leaves could be found, together with a fiery dragon, pterodactyls, owls, bats and caterpillars. The trees and street lamps were strung with fairy lamps and chinese lanterns.

The main parade was full of little stalls, not only selling refreshments and ice-cream but an array of Festival souvenirs such as ash trays, decanters, glasses, jugs, teapots, spoons, badges, tie-pins, and even horse-brasses, all with the Festival logo. The Gothic towers, painted red and 65 feet high, were crowned with dovecotes.

Rowland Emmett also designed the Shell ByPlane X100, with a pilot named Professor Septimus Urge at the controls. This impossible craft was powered by rocket, balloon, steam, sail, muscle-power and had many safety features, including lifebelt, weather vane, umbrella, oil lamps and an anchor.

The Festival showboat, built on wooden piles over the Thames, had a series of tableau displays that included Jonah and the Whale, Atlantis and a display entitled Under the Icecap.

The Far Tottering station on the Emmett railway gave the impression of a quietly collapsing country halt needing the odd repairs. Fares were 1s 6d adult return or 9d for children. The railway was dismantled and removed in 1954.

Feeding seagulls, Chelsea Bridge, c. 1910.